Heinemann
LIBRARY

Chicago, Illinois

Behind the News | **HUMAN RIGHTS:**
Who Decides**?**

A N N
K R A M E R

© 2007 Heinemann Library
a division of Reed Elsevier Inc.
Chicago, Illinois

Customer Service 888-454-2279
Visit our website at www.heinemannraintree.com

Designed by David Poole and Kamae Design
Printed and bound in China by South China
Printing Company

11 10 09 08 07
10 9 8 7 6 5 4 3 2 1

**Library of Congress Cataloging-in-Publication
Data**
Kramer, Ann.
  Human rights : who decides? / Ann Kramer.
      p. cm. -- (Behind the news)
  Includes bibliographical references and index.
  ISBN 1-4034-8832-0 (lib. bdg.)
  1-4034-9352-9 (pbk.)
  1. Human rights--Juvenile literature. I. Title. II.
Series: Behind the news (Chicago, Ill.)
  JC571.K645 2006
  323--dc22
                                    2006017503

The paper used to print this book comes from
sustainable resources.

Disclaimer
All the Internet addresses (URLs) given in this
book were valid at the time of going to press.
However, due to the dynamic nature of the
Internet, some addresses may have changed, or
sites may have ceased to exist since publication.
While the author and publishers regret any
inconvenience this may cause readers, no
responsibility for any such changes can be
accepted by either the author or the publishers.

Acknowledgments
The publishers would like to thank the following
for permission to reproduce photographs:
Amnesty International p. 12; Corbis pp. 10
(Corbis/Bettmann), 13 (Fehim Demir/Epa), 15
(David Turnley), 17 (Hulton Deutsch), 25
(Benjamin Lowy), 27 (Shaun Best/Reuters), 31
(Barry Lewis), 33 (Charles Platiau/Reuters), 36
(Reuters), 37 (Ricki Rosen), 38 (B. Neumann/
Zefa), 47 (Reuters), 48 (Reuters); Empics pp. 5
(AP), 18 (AP), 40 (AP), 44 (AP); Getty Images pp.
6, 16, 21 (AFP), 22 (AFP), 24, 35 (Getty Images),
49 (Photodisc); Magnum pp. 29 (Alex Majoli), 43
(Thomas Dworzak); NSPCC p. 39; Topfoto pp. 7
(Imageworks), 11.

Cover photograph of a victim of torture,
reproduced with permission of Corbis (Patrick
Robert).

The author and Publishers gratefully acknowledge
the publications from which the longer written
sources in the book are drawn. In some cases
the wording or sentence structure has been
simplified to make the material appropriate for
a school readership:

Arie Farnum (in the *Christian Science Monitor*)
p.30; the *Independent* p.37.

Every effort has been made to contact copyright
holders of any material reproduced in this book.
Any omissions will be rectified in subsequent
printings if notice is given to the publishers.

CONTENTS

Any words appearing in the text in bold, **like this**, are explained in the Glossary.

CAGED LIKE ANIMALS: GUANTÁNAMO

"Camp X-Ray Pictures Spark Outrage"

On January 11, 2002, 20 prisoners from Afghanistan arrived at the U.S. military outpost in Guantánamo Bay, Cuba. They had been taken to Guantánamo to be **interrogated** about **al-Qaeda** networks and Osama bin Laden. The U.S. government believed al-Qaeda and bin Laden had carried out the September 11, 2001, terrorist attacks on New York and the Pentagon. By 2005 Guantánamo Bay had held up to 600 prisoners without trial. Many of the prisoners had not been charged with any specific offense.

Newspapers around the world featured dramatic headlines and images of the prisoners arriving at Camp X-Ray in Guantánamo Bay in hoods and shackles. U.S. marines and military police herded the prisoners into tiny cage-like cells.

The **media** also reported a range of opinions about the prisoners. Human rights organizations, such as **Amnesty International**, protested against the "cruel treatment" of the prisoners. One source described the prisoners as "bound and gagged, drugged, caged like animals."

Others justified the harsh treatment. According to Marine Brigadier General Mike Lehnert, commander of Joint Task Force 160, which was overseeing the operation, the prisoners were "the worst elements of al-Qaeda and the **Taliban** . . . the bad guys." He said their treatment would be "humane but not comfortable." U.S. President George W. Bush said the prisoners were "killers" who "don't share the same values we share."

"Human rights scandal" or justifiable detention?

What is the story behind these reports? The situation of the prisoners at Guantánamo Bay has always been controversial. Their detention has caused an international outcry. Controversy has focused on the status and rights of the prisoners. The Bush **administration** has said the prisoners are "**unlawful combatants**." This means they do not have rights that would normally be granted to other prisoners—particularly those captured in war. They are also being held in Cuba, which means they do not have the right to be brought in front of a U.S. judge and told the charges against them. This process—called habeas corpus—is a fundamental **constitutional** right in the United States. The prisoners would have this right if they were held in the United States.

Amnesty International has called Guantánamo Bay a "human rights scandal" and says the prisoners remain in a "legal black hole . . . denied their rights under international law." U.S. Defense Secretary Donald Rumsfeld has defended the situation, however, saying: "There are among these prisoners people who are perfectly willing to kill themselves and kill other people. Unlawful combatants do not have any rights under the **Geneva Convention**."

Who decides?

Do the prisoners at Guantánamo Bay have the right to a fair trial, access to lawyers, and the right of appeal? Or, given their **alleged** connection to the terrorist attacks, are they not allowed these human rights? Who should decide?

Dressed in orange jumpsuits and often shackled, hundreds of prisoners have been held at Guantánamo. There have been allegations in the media that prisoners have been tortured.

Defining human rights

When we open a newspaper or switch on the television, we often see someone talking about, or campaigning for, human rights. The issue of human rights is one of the most important today, but what does it mean?

Human rights are said to be the rights we have simply because we are human beings. They have been described as:

- Inalienable: They cannot be taken away
- Indivisible: Equally important
- Interdependent: All part of an interlocking framework of rights.

Most of us believe we have certain rights. We expect freedom from **discrimination** and the right to be treated equally no matter what our gender, age, skin color, ethnic group, religious belief, or sexual orientation. These rights can be described as basic human rights.

Rights may be civil and political—the right to vote, for instance. They can also be economic, social, and cultural—for example, the right to a fair wage or an education. Ideally our rights cannot be taken and are protected by law, but this is not always the case.

In April 1994 black South Africans were able to vote for the first time. Many people believe the right to vote and be treated equally are fundamental human rights. Under **apartheid** (1948–c.1991) black South Africans were deprived of human rights because they were not believed to be equal with white people.

Are human rights universal?

In some countries, human rights have been written into **constitutions** and are part of the laws of that country. They are often known as **civil rights**. There are also many countries that do not recognize basic human rights, or that allow one group of people more rights than others.

Some people argue there can be no such thing as universal human rights because of differences in cultural, religious, and political beliefs around the world. Something that is considered a human right in one part of the world cannot necessarily be imposed elsewhere. Many countries—particularly in Asia and the Middle East—have criticized human rights as being too **biased** toward Western beliefs and values.

A complex issue

The issue of human rights is complex and controversial. It gives rise to many questions, such as: Who decides what a right is or should be? Are all people equal, regardless of gender or race, and should they all have the same rights? Are the rights of groups of people more important than the rights of individuals? Are some rights more important than others? For instance, is the right to food, shelter, and work more important than the right to vote?

Very importantly, how can human rights be protected, and how can the abuse of human rights be prevented?

The right to peaceful protest is a basic human right. Some people claim it is a fundamental right in **democracies**. There are many countries, however, in which protest is forbidden or controlled.

The Universal Declaration of Human Rights

In 1948 the United Nations (UN) published the Universal Declaration of Human Rights. It was aspirational rather than legal, which means the rights were something that nations should be aiming to provide for citizens, but the the rights did not actually exist in law. The Declaration listed human rights that ought to be enjoyed by every human being. The Declaration is made up of a **preamble** and 30 sections, known as articles. The first 15 articles cover civil and political rights; articles 16 to 30 cover economic, social, and cultural rights.

The text below has been simplified and shortened. You can read the full declaration on http://www.un.org/Overview/rights.html.

THE DECLARATION:

Preamble

Dignity, equality, and inalienable rights of all members of the human family are the foundation of freedom, justice, and peace. The General Assembly [of the United Nations] proclaims this Universal Declaration of Human Rights as a common standard of achievement for all peoples and all nations . . .

Article 1: All human beings are born free and equal in dignity and rights . . . and should act towards one another in a spirit of brotherhood.

Article 2: Everyone, no matter what their race, color, sex, language, religion, political belief, or status is entitled to all the rights and freedoms in this Declaration.

Article 3: Everyone has the right to life, liberty, and personal security.

Article 4: No one shall be held in slavery or servitude.

Article 5: No one shall be tortured or subject to cruel, inhuman, or degrading treatment or punishment.

Article 6: Everyone, no matter where they are, has the right to be recognized as a person by law.

Article 7: Everyone is equal before the law and has the right to equal legal protection, without discrimination.

Article 8: Everyone has the right to seek legal help if his or her human rights are **violated**.

Article 9: No one shall be subjected to arbitrary arrest, detention, or exile without due legal process.

Article 10: Everyone charged with a crime is entitled to a fair trial by an independent court.

Article 11: Everyone charged with a crime is entitled to be presumed innocent until proven guilty.

Article 12: No one should be subjected to interference with his or her privacy, family, home, or correspondence.

Article 13: Everyone has the right to live where they want and move freely within their own country. Everyone has the right to leave and return to his or her country.

Article 14: Everyone has the right to seek **asylum** in another country if they are being persecuted. This does not apply if someone has been charged with a crime such as murder, or anything that conflicts with the spirit of the United Nations.

Article 15: Everyone has the right to a nationality.

Article 16: Men and women have the right to marry and start a family. The family is entitled to be protected by society.

Article 17: Everyone has the right to own property and the right not to be deprived of his or her property.

Article 18: Everyone has the right to freedom of thought, conscience, and religion.

Article 19: Everyone has the right to freedom of thought and speech.

Article 20: Everyone has the right to freedom of peaceful assembly and association.

Article 21: Everyone has the right to take part in the government of his or her country, directly or through representatives, i.e. the right to vote and elect representatives. [This is often defined as the right to democracy.]

Article 22: Everyone has the right to economic, social, and cultural security.

Article 23: Everyone has the right to work; to equal pay for equal work; and the right to join a trade union.

Article 24: Everyone has the right to rest, leisure, and holidays.

Article 25: Everyone has the right to an adequate standard of living.

Article 26: Everyone has the right to an education. Parents are entitled to choose education for their children.

Article 27: Everyone has the right to take part in the cultural life of his or her community.

Article 28: Everyone is entitled to live in a situation where the rights and freedoms of this Declaration can be realized.

Article 29: Everyone has a duty to serve and support his or her community. An individual's rights can be limited in order to protect the rights and freedoms of others.

Article 30: No one should act in any way that will damage the rights and freedoms of another person.

The development of human rights

The idea that each of us is entitled to rights because we are human is fairly recent. It was the **atrocities** of World War II (1939–1945) that really led to the development of universal human rights.

The Holocaust

The horrors of World War II shocked the world. Those who were responsible for the extermination of more than six million Jews, as well as the murder of **Roma**, homosexuals, and others in the Holocaust, were brought to trial at Nuremberg, Germany. This was a key event in the development of human rights. For the first time, it showed the world that those who caused death and suffering on such a scale could and would be tried and punished.

Never again

After the war there was an overwhelming wish to make sure such atrocities never happened again. In 1945 the United Nations was created to encourage peace, security, and international cooperation. The founding nations wanted to establish human rights standards to protect citizens from being abused by their governments. The preamble to the UN Declaration of Human Rights called it "a common standard of achievement for all people and all nations."

The 1946 trial at Nuremberg of Nazi leaders for "crimes against humanity" was a landmark in human rights development. For the first time, an international court was set up to try individuals who had committed atrocities against the citizens of their own country.

The Universal Declaration

The UN set up a Commission on Human Rights, which drafted and produced a document listing universal human rights. On December 10, 1948, the Universal Declaration of Human Rights (see pp. 8–9) was issued and approved by 48 member states. Eight member states refused to vote.

The declaration established the principle that how a government treats its citizens is a matter of international concern, not just a national issue. The declaration was not legally binding, but it has been very influential. Many countries have included its principles in their constitutions. Some people say it has the status of **customary international law**, since it is used in custom rather than being a written law. Others disagree.

Treaties and conventions

Following the declaration, the UN drafted two treaties, each with the aim of enforcing human rights: the International Covenant on Civil and Political Rights (ICCPR) and the International Covenant on Economic, Social, and Cultural Rights (ICESCR). They came into force in 1976. Since then, more than 140 countries have **ratified** (accepted) them.

As chair of the UN Commission on Human Rights, Eleanor Roosevelt (1884–1962) helped to draft the Universal Declaration of Human Rights. She was the wife of President Franklin D. Roosevelt (1933–45).

Since 1948 the UN has adopted many treaties, covenants, and conventions on differing human rights, some of which are now part of international law. They include conventions to prevent and outlaw torture and **genocide** and to protect the rights of vulnerable groups such as women, **refugees**, and children.

HUMAN RIGHTS DOCUMENTS

Regional groups have produced their own documents for the protection and promotion of human rights. For example:

- In 1950 the European Council produced the European Convention on Human Rights, which came into force in 1953
- In 1981 African states produced a Charter of Human and Peoples' Rights
- In 1990 Muslim states created the Cairo Declaration on Human Rights in Islam.

Human rights movement

From the 1960s a new human rights movement emerged. Hundreds of non-governmental organizations (NGOs) sprang up. They included Amnesty International, Human Rights Watch, and many others. These organizations were made up of ordinary citizens, rather than government officials, and they highlighted and promoted human rights. They campaigned on a range of human rights issues and worked to raise awareness of human rights nationally and internationally.

Individual voices

Many individuals helped to raise the banner of human rights. Some notable campaigners included South African Nelson Mandela, who fought apartheid in South Africa, and Czech Václav Havel, who campaigned for reform of the communist regime. Groups such as Tibetan monks and Ecuadorian farmers also fought for their human rights to be recognized. By the end of the 20th century, there was human rights activity everywhere.

What was achieved?

There is disagreement about how much has actually been achieved in the field of human rights since 1948. Some say very little has been achieved because, despite treaties and conventions, human rights violations continue. Others point to some successes, particularly in South Africa, the overthrow of communist regimes, and the high profile of human rights.

The **Cold War** dominated international politics from 1948 to 1991. Although the "superpowers" were not at war, conflicts and even genocide continued. China seized control of Tibet, Pol Pot's regime slaughtered 1.7 million people in Cambodia, and numerous people "disappeared" under repressive regimes

in South America. Apartheid ruled in South Africa, and Indonesia oppressed the island of East Timor. Their actions have all **contravened** international law.

Meanwhile, the UN seemed powerless or unwilling to prevent human rights violations. One reason for this was the idea of sovereignty: nations should not interfere in the business of other nations.

The Amnesty International symbol represents light (the candle) being shed on human rights abuses (the barbed wire).

However, there were also positive developments. For example, international pressure helped to end the apartheid regime in South Africa. In 1989 many countries in the Soviet Union were inspired by the idea of human rights. They worked to overthrow the regimes supported by the Soviet Union and introduced more democratic forms of government.

Recent developments

Since the 1990s there have been other important developments in human rights. After years of human rights abuse in East Timor and Kosovo, UN-led troops and NATO forces invaded. A number of the world's leaders were charged with human rights abuses or crimes against humanity. They included the former Chilean president, General Augusto Pinochet, and the Serbian military leader Ratko Mladic. In 1998 proposals were put in place for an International Criminal Court where abuses of human rights could be tried. Many nations have ratified it, although seven nations, including China, Saudi Arabia, Libya, and the United States, have opposed it.

A new challenge

It has been argued that increasing terrorist activity—particularly the attacks on September 11, 2001—present a new challenge to human rights. There are concerns that democratic societies, particularly the United States, may introduce measures to combat terrorism that infringe or sidestep **civil liberties** and human rights. For example, human rights advocates are concerned that proposed anti-terrorism **legislation**, such as laws increasing the amount of time a suspected terrorist may have to stay in prison before being charged, represents a violation of human rights. Some also argue that new laws directed at preventing the "glorification" of terrorism may be used against a wide variety of groups that are not involved in terrorism at all.

In July 1995 nearly 8,000 Bosnian men were slaughtered by a Serbian army under General Ratko Mladic. Many people want to know why the massacre was not prevented.

Rwanda: 100 days of killing

In 1994 the central African country of Rwanda experienced one of the worst human rights abuses in modern times. Rwanda is home to two ethnic groups: the Hutu, who make up more than 80 percent of the population, and the much smaller group of Tutsis. Tensions between the two groups have been a feature of the country's history.

In 1994 tensions flared into violence. From April to July 1994 a massacre occurred in Rwanda. In just 100 days, Hutu militia massacred an estimated 800,000 Tutsis and some moderate Hutus. Yet there were very few newspaper headlines about it. Early media reporting was nonexistent or contradictory, and no one got involved to stop the massacre.

Non-intervention

Why did no one intervene? The UN had received advance warning that the Hutu government was planning a massacre. UN peacekeeping forces were in the region. Canadian Lieutenant General Roméo Dallaire, leader of the peacekeeping forces, asked for permission to intervene, but the UN refused. They said his forces had a monitoring role only. In contrast to his request, the Security Council withdrew most of the peacekeeping forces. French, Belgian, and U.S. citizens were also removed from Rwanda.

Rwanda had a seat on the UN Security Council. Its ambassador insisted the killings were exaggerated. In contrast, Kenneth Roth, of the Human Rights Watch organization, wrote to the UN and called the killings genocide. He urged intervention to "prevent and punish the perpetrators" in line with international law. Despite this, the UN and United States did not define the killings as genocide. The UN Security Council passed a resolution condemning the killings, but did not use the word "genocide." U.S. President Bill Clinton said he was "shocked and horrified that elements of the Rwanda security forces . . . sought out and murdered Rwandan officials" and called "on all parties to cease." His administration defined the conflict as "black on black" violence. British and other diplomats referred to "tribal hatreds" and said the violence was a "breakdown in the ceasefire agreement." This ceasefire, to end a long-running civil war between the Hutus and Tutsis, had been agreed to in 1993.

The massacre in Rwanda has been called one of the worst crimes in recent history. It is now defined as genocide, but was not described that way at the time. Both former President Clinton and Kofi Annan, Secretary General of the UN, have since apologized for not doing more.

Criticisms of the UN and United States

Following the massacre, reports in the international media criticized the UN and United States for not preventing or ending the tragedy. Some suggested that the United States opposed intervention because it had made a disastrous intervention in Somalia the previous year, which had cost U.S. lives. One commentator said failure to intervene was "because the problems of a small country in central Africa were of no strategic concern." Rwandan President Paul Kagame said: "I would hate to believe that this agenda is dictated by **racist** considerations. I hope it is not true."

By mid-May 1994 the UN Security Council had said that "acts of genocide may have been committed" and agreed to send 5,500 troops to Rwanda. The deployment of troops was delayed, however, because of arguments over who was to cover the costs. Madeline Albright, the U.S. representative to the UN, said: "The United States has been a driving force in the provision of humanitarian assistance [but] . . . sending a UN force into the maelstrom [turbulent situation] of Rwanda without a sound plan . . . would be folly [foolish] . . . ultimately, the future of Rwanda is in Rwandan hands."

Who was right?

If the United States and UN had defined the massacre as genocide, they would have been legally obliged to intervene. Some military experts have said that military intervention would have prevented hundreds, if not thousands, of deaths. At the time, the United States and the UN argued it was not genocide and that Rwandans needed to sort out their own problems.

Reporting human rights

The media plays a key role in highlighting and reporting human rights events. It informs and helps to shape public opinion. As events unfold, we get the latest images, commentaries, and opinions. Do we always get the truth?

Confusion and contradiction

Genocide is difficult to report. Rwanda is an example of this. At first the media did not pick up on the event. BBC reporter Tom Giles said: "For nearly three weeks in April . . . the story of one of the 20th century's worst crimes had failed . . . to make the top of the TV news bulletins."

There were various reasons. At that time the media focus was on the first-ever multiracial election in South Africa. Information about Rwanda was confusing; at first the media did not realize the extent of the killings. They reported far smaller numbers and suggested that the killings were part of an ongoing "tribal" civil war.

Images were too shocking to show. The country was dangerous and journalists were forced to leave. It was not safe to return once the UN had gone.

After the massacre was over, the media carried reports criticizing the UN and the United States for non-intervention. However, some human rights organizations have said "erratic media coverage . . . [meant] . . . there was little public pressure in the West for governments to intervene."

Zimbabwean journalist Sandra Nyaira (left) is one of many who have been forced into exile by President Mugabe's government because they attempted to report human rights abuses in Zimbabwe.

Australian John Pilger is a campaigning journalist who has written extensively on human rights. He produced television documentaries on Cambodia and the plight of the East Timorese, which drew public attention to human abuses that were being ignored.

Differing perspectives

Newspapers present different **slants** on the same event, depending on their bias. A politically conservative newspaper may interpret an event quite differently from a liberal newspaper. National or regional media may also have different opinions and editorial policies. The perspective of the Arab news network al-Jazeera may not be the same as the *Washington Post*. During the *Tampa* refugee crisis in Australia (see pp. 34–35), Australian newspapers defended the right of Australia to refuse asylum to refugees. Newspapers elsewhere attacked this. Media reports include opposing opinions. Finding the truth behind these opinions can be difficult.

Media reports can arouse strong feelings. Discussing media coverage of asylum seekers or refugees, Australian journalist Peter Mares has said: "Media reporting can shape public perception . . . compassionate and sympathetic coverage can help to promote public understanding . . . negative reporting can generate and intensify feelings of fear."

The media is an important channel of information about human rights. It can be used to carry accurate reports and open discussion or for **propaganda**. Getting to the truth may mean digging through many different reports.

The stories no one wants told

Human rights events do not always reach the media. Freedom of the press is an important human right, and most democracies support this, most of the time. Repressive regimes do not encourage it. Countries such as Uzbekistan, Zimbabwe, and China, for instance, have **censored** press coverage of their regimes. Many journalists who have attempted to cover human rights abuses have been forced into exile, imprisoned, or killed.

Enforcing human rights

It's one thing to create human rights—enforcing them is another. What happens if a human right becomes law, but governments or rulers do not abide by it? How can human rights be enforced?

International human rights law: The process

For human rights to be legally binding, they must be written into documents called conventions (also known as treaties or covenants). These set international standards. When a government signs a convention, it becomes legally bound to uphold these standards.

Before conventions become law, they must be:

- Drafted by working groups: These include representatives of member states and NGOs
- Adopted by a vote of the UN General Assembly
- Signed by member states: This not only shows that a member state is beginning the legal process, but also implies that it will refrain from abusing that right
- Ratified by member states: This signifies that the member state intends to follow the provisions laid out in the document. There is an opportunity for the state to express concerns about the contents of the convention.
- Entered into force: It becomes law when a minimum of 35 member states have ratified it.

The process of creating international human rights law can take many years, and there is no guarantee that all member states will agree. As new human rights are recognized and defined, international law develops to meet the need.

A member of the Kashmiri All Party Hurriyat (Freedom) Conference takes part in a hunger strike on International Human Rights Day in Jammu, India. Many Kashmiris are demanding their right to independence.

Enforcing rights

There are human rights courts to enforce human rights, notably the European Court of Human Rights in Strasbourg, France, and the International Criminal Court (ICC). The ICC is the first permanent international criminal court, but various major countries, including the United States, Libya, Saudi Arabia, and China, do not recognize its powers.

In theory, the UN should be able to enforce human rights. Some say it has failed. Even after signing the UN declaration and numerous treaties, member states do not necessarily uphold or enforce human rights. Member states may not agree with each other, or they may have political or economic reasons for ignoring violations taking place in another country.

Does one country have the right to enforce human rights on another? This is probably one of the most controversial issues. Is there any country in the world where human rights are so respected that the country can make that decision? What happens when a country with a good human rights record infringes human rights in some areas?

The continuing debate

Some people argue that there is no single way to enforce human rights. Treaties are in place, but effective procedures for enforcing them are still to be found. The debate continues, and it is still unclear who makes the decisions.

Pressure to enforce human rights can take many forms, including diplomacy, lobbying and political protest, and **economic sanctions**. Armed intervention is another highly controversial method. Some say that those who violate human rights should be isolated. Others think that they must be included in the world community and will learn by example.

China is an example of this difference of opinion. Its record on human rights is poor. Censorship, torture, and political repression there are well documented. In 2008 China will stage the Olympic Games in Beijing. The International Olympics Committee (IOC) made this decision, and China celebrated. Human rights advocates, however, were horrified. Some said that China's record on human rights violates the spirit of the Olympics and should disqualify them. Others have argued that the international focus on China will force the Chinese government to do more to uphold human rights in that country.

The death penalty

The right to life is the most fundamental human right of all—or is it? The death penalty is legal in many countries, including China, Iran, and the United States.

Napoleon Beazley

In 2002 a 25-year-old African American, Napoleon Beazley, was executed by lethal injection in Texas for a murder he had committed when he was 17. In 1994, while stealing a car with two friends, Beazley shot the car's owner dead. Beazley was found guilty and sentenced to death in 1995. He spent six years on death row while his case went through a number of ultimately unsuccessful appeals.

High-profile focus

Executions often become high-profile media stories. The case of Napoleon Beazley was no exception. Media reports became more detailed as the execution approached. The case attracted widespread criticism. The Council of Europe called for a review. Amnesty International said: "The U.S. undermines its own claims to be a progressive force for human rights." South African Archbishop Desmond Tutu said: "I am astounded that Texas and a few other states in the United States take children from their families and execute them."

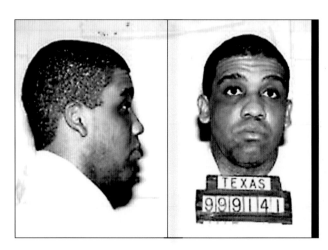

The world's media focused on Napoleon Beazley, who was executed in Texas in 2002. In the United States in January 2006, 3,373 prisoners were on death row, awaiting execution.

LANDMARK DECISION

On March 1, 2005, the U.S. Supreme Court abolished the death penalty for those who commit murder when they are younger than 18. The court acknowledged the "overwhelming weight of international opinion."

Beazley's defense lawyer said the sentence was "contrary to international law" and "violated human rights, particularly the rights of children." Beazley, who was just over three months away from his 18th birthday when he committed the murder, was a juvenile. The Convention on the Rights of the Child prohibits anyone under 18 from being sentenced to death or executed. However, under Texas law at the time, Beazley was considered an adult and could therefore be sentenced to death.

The defense lawyer claimed that the prosecution evidence was flawed, and that the all-white jury was racially prejudiced. He said Beazley was being penalized because the victim was a well-known businessman and his son a federal judge. The prosecution denied these claims. One attorney accused the defense lawyer of "having a political ax to grind" and ignoring the distress of the victim's family. He described Napoleon Beazley as a "vicious murderer."

Police chiefs said Beazley was a "cold-blooded killer." The district attorney defended the death penalty because the murder was "random" and "predatory." He said: "Napoleon Beazley is a threat to society. There is no way he deserves anything less than the death penalty . . . he is an adult under Texas law."

DEATH PENALTY WORLDWIDE

According to Amnesty International:
- Seventy-five countries retain capital punishment, also known as the death penalty, on their statute (law) books but do not necessarily carry it out
- In 2005, 18 countries carried out the death penalty. China, Iran, Vietnam, and the United States between them accounted for 97 percent of all known executions.
- China leads the death penalty figures, having executed at least 3,400 people in 2004. Iran executed 159, Vietnam 64 people, and the United States 59.
- Capital punishment (under **Sharia** law) is used in most Muslim countries for various offenses, including murder, drug **trafficking**, adultery (cheating on one's spouse), and rape. In China it is used for around 60 offenses, ranging from murder to corruption. In most of the other countries, including the United States, it is used mainly to punish murder. A few states retain the death penalty for other crimes, such as treason (attempting to overturn or harm one's own country), rape, kidnapping with violence, and aircraft hijacking.

For and against: Who decides?

Capital punishment arouses strong emotions. There is no overarching international law banning the death penalty. Nations make their own decisions. In the United States, individual states decide whether or not to use it.

Those who defend capital punishment say it is a **deterrent**. They believe it is an appropriate or "fair" punishment because people who take life should have their life taken from them. They say someone who murders another has forfeited (given up) his or her human rights.

Opponents say capital punishment is a fundamental violation of human rights and should not be used by any "civilized" society. They argue that capital punishment is not a deterrent because, for example, murder rates remain high in the United States. Mistakes also occur, causing innocent people to be executed. They also claim sentencing is racially biased: proportionally more African Americans are executed than white Americans.

"A bitter moral and legal tug of war"

This quote from CNN was used to describe the human rights case of Terri Schiavo—but what was the story behind the news?

CHANGING OPINIONS

According to The Death Penalty Information Center, public opinion in the United States is changing:

- 1994: 80 percent supported the death penalty
- 2005: 64 percent supported the death penalty
- 1994: 32 percent supported life imprisonment without parole
- 2004: 46 percent supported life imprisonment without parole

In 2005 President George W. Bush reaffirmed his support for the death penalty, saying: "Ultimately it helps save innocent lives."

Chinese police take a man away to be executed. He was found guilty of poisoning 70 children. Amnesty International and other human rights organizations have called for a worldwide ban on capital punishment.

Fierce legal battle

From 1998 to 2005 a fierce legal battle took place in the United States. A Florida woman, Terri Schiavo, suffered a heart attack in 1990 that left her with severe brain damage. Schiavo was in what is known as a **persistent vegetative state (PVS)**. She could not eat or swallow and was kept alive with a feeding tube. Her husband, Michael, wanted the tube removed, allowing her to die. He said that would have been her wish, although she had not left written instructions. Her parents, Robert and Mary Schindler, argued their daughter could be treated and had the right to live.

Michael Schiavo and the Schindlers fought each other through the U.S. courts. There were 14 appeals. Florida Governor Jeb Bush and President George W. Bush intervened, opposing the removal of the feeding tube. The Florida Supreme Court supported the husband. Terri Schiavo's feeding tube was removed on March 18, 2005. She died on March 31.

The right to die

Article 3 of the Universal Declaration of Human rights states: "Everyone has the right to life." But can the "right to die" also be a human right? Family members, medical practitioners, and pro-life and right-to-die advocates aired opposing views through newspapers, on television, and on the Internet.

CNN described the case as "one of the nation's longest and most contentious right-to-die cases." Harvard law professor Laurence Tribe was quoted by CNN: "I've never seen a case in which the state legislature treats someone's life as a political football in quite the way this is being done."

U.S. lawyer and environmentalist Ralph Nader, disability groups, and others attacked the decision to remove the feeding tube as a violation of Terri Schiavo's human rights. The New York newspaper *Village Voice* ran a front-page article headed "Terri Schiavo: Judicial Murder." It stated that "a 41-year-old woman, who has committed no crime, will die of dehydration and starvation in the longest public execution in American history." The article claimed Terri Schiavo's **due process** rights had been violated.

In contrast, ABC News ran a poll claiming 63 percent of the U.S. public supported the removal of Schiavo's feeding tube. Medical ethics expert Peter A. Clark stated that "a number of eminent neurologists" had confirmed Schiavo was in a persistent vegetative state and her husband "had the ethical and legal right to withdraw or withhold treatment."

Who decides?

According to Jay Wolfson, Professor of Public Health and Medicine at the University of South Florida: "The basis for the decisions regarding Theresa Schiavo were firmly grounded within Florida statutory and case law, which clearly and unequivocally provide for the removal of artificial nutrition in cases of persistent vegetative states."

The media reports indicated that even though the law allowed for the removal of the feeding tube, there were opposing views. Terri Schiavo's husband and lawyer talked of Schiavo's "right to die in peace and dignity." Her parents wanted her "right" to continued life. There were arguments that removing the feeding tube would mean Schiavo would starve to death painfully.

Who is right? Many people feel they would rather die than live in pain or in a vegetative state. Should people have the right to decide when and how they die? Should other people—family, courts, politicians, or doctors—be allowed to make that decision? In this case, was it correct to allow Terri Schiavo to starve to death, or was there another way? Can the right to die ever be universal?

The case of Terri Schiavo made media headlines throughout the United States and around the world. As medical technology keeps people alive for longer, the right-to-die debate is intensifying.

Torture takes many forms, including the use of electric shock, dousing with water, cigarette burns, beating, and depriving a person of sleep, food, and security. Even if people recover physically from torture, they continue to suffer from anxiety, depression, insecurity, and flashbacks.

Torture by proxy

Torture is defined as the "intentional infliction of severe mental or physical pain or suffering for a specific purpose." It is regarded as a brutal human rights abuse—but can it ever be justified?

Illegal and prohibited

Article 5 of the UN declaration states: "No one shall be tortured or given cruel, inhuman or degrading punishments." Torture is illegal under international law. Since World War II, governments worldwide have agreed to ban torture. By 2004 more than 130 countries had ratified the Convention Against Torture. Individual countries, too, had passed their own laws banning torture.

Despite these bans, estimates suggest that more than 150 countries still use torture. Most countries that use torture are those with a poor record of human rights. They include China, Egypt, Iran, Yemen, Syria, and Uzbekistan, where torture is routinely carried out as a means of social control. Recent reports suggest that Western democracies have also been **colluding** in torture. There are allegations that they are transferring people suspected of being terrorists to countries where they are likely to be tortured.

OPPOSING VIEWS

One senior FBI agent has said: "If I knew the man in front of me had critical information that would prevent a catastrophic attack on the USA, I would torture him and take the consequences. Wouldn't you?"

Kofi Annan has said: "Torture can never be an instrument to fight terror, for torture is an instrument of terror."

Extraordinary rendition: Torture by proxy

In 2002 Maher Arar, a Syrian-born Canadian citizen, was detained at Kennedy International Airport by U.S. immigration officials. His name appeared on a terrorist watch list. He was questioned and then put on a private plane to Syria, where he was interrogated and tortured for 10 months. He was eventually released after it was established that he had no links to terrorist groups. The Canadian government lodged an official complaint with the U.S. government.

Maher Arar's situation was widely reported in the media as an example of what is known as **extraordinary rendition**. This is when a country where torture is illegal, such as the United States, transfers (renders) a terror suspect to another country where it is allowed. It is also known as "torture by proxy," because it is alleged that security forces in another country torture a suspect on behalf of the first country. The case of Maher Arar was one headline case, but the media and human rights advocates have highlighted many others.

Claims and counter-claims

In February 2005 a report in the *New Yorker* claimed that since 2001, the United States has "rendered" around 150 people suspected of terrorist activities. The *Washington Post* claimed terrorist suspects were being transferred to secret detention centers around the world. The prisoners were then interrogated using techniques, such as torture, that are prohibited in the United States.

In the United Kingdom, the *Guardian* newspaper suggested the British government was also involved and would be "guilty of breaking international law if it knowingly allowed secret CIA 'rendition' flights to land at UK airports."

The Bush administration has not denied rendition, but says it makes every attempt to ensure that countries to which suspects are rendered do not use torture. When President Bush was challenged on the issue in 2005, he said: "In a post 9/11 world the United States must make sure we protect our people and our friends from attack . . . one way to do it is to arrest people and send them back to their country of origin, with the promise they won't be tortured. This country does not believe in torture. We do believe in protecting ourselves."

In December 2005 the *Guardian* reported that U.S. Secretary of State Condoleezza Rice refused to confirm or deny the existence of CIA-run secret prisons. She defended the CIA's use of "rendition" because information gathered had "prevented terrorist attacks in Europe . . . and other countries." She stated: "The U.S. does not transport, and has not transported, detainees from one country to another for the purpose of interrogation using torture."

Do ends justify means?

Torture is brutal. Can it ever be justified? Can it be used in extraordinary circumstances—for instance, to detect and prevent possible terrorist attacks? These questions have become more pressing since the September 11, 2001, terrorist attack on New York and the more recent bombings in Madrid and London. Many people fear there will be further attacks. Security forces, such as the FBI and CIA, argue that torture can be justified if it produces information that will prevent an attack. Other people disagree. They say that torture is one of the worst abuses of human rights, that it is illegal, and that a person being tortured will say anything to stop it from happening, so that information may not be reliable anyway. What do you think?

Syrian-born Canadian citizen Maher Arar was deported to Syria in 2002. His family was not told where he was. He returned a year later saying he had been tortured, and he accused the United States of collusion.

EQUAL RIGHTS

Is everyone equal?
The first and second articles of the UN declaration state that all people are born free and have equal rights; all people should have the same human rights, no matter what their sex, race, religion, political belief, and so on. The message is clear, but are all people treated equally?

Women's rights
During the 20th century, women worldwide campaigned for their right to have a political voice and be treated equally with men. Many advances were made, and today women in many societies have achieved equal status in law, if not always in practice. Women's rights are far from universal, however, and many claim there are places where women are treated as second-class citizens.

No votes for women
Saudi Arabia is an absolute monarchy, meaning its royal family can enforce any laws it wishes. Saudi Arabia is governed by Sharia law. Sharia (Islamic) law is open to many interpretations, but it does not generally encourage women to hold prominent positions. In 2005 Saudi Arabia held its first nationwide municipal elections. Women, who make up more than 50 percent of the population, did not take part. They were not allowed to vote or to run as candidates.

Differing reasons
Human rights groups and the media, including CBS, *Arab News*, the BBC, and al-Jazeera, covered the election and the reasons for excluding women. Views differed . . .

The BBC stated that Saudi women had been "barred" from voting. Amnesty International claimed the exclusion of women from the election was "based on gender" and violated the UN Convention on the Elimination of All Forms of Discrimination Against Women (CEDAW). This convention requires women to be given the vote and has been signed by Saudi Arabia.

Arab News quoted a senior election official who said the reason was "administrative." Prince Mansour ibn Miteb expressed his hope that women would vote in new elections due in 2009, but said: "Municipal elections are a new experience in the kingdom and the short time given to the Election Commission made it impossible to allow women's participation." Another official said that the election bylaw did not exclude women from voting, but there were not enough women to run voter registration centers and only a few women had photo identity cards.

WHOSE DECISION IS IT?

The Bush administration stated it was "disappointed that women were not permitted to participate." The United States and Saudi Arabia are close allies.

Arab News reported an independent poll of 240 Saudis, which showed that 87 percent supported women taking part in the election. Some Saudi women welcomed the poll and were happy to see the survey. Others doubted that it actually reflected the real views of Saudis. Some said it did not represent the whole population, and that only people "belonging to a certain educated class" had been surveyed. Rasha Muhamad, an employee of the Girl's Education Department, said: "I do not think the general Saudi public shares this feeling." Another woman, Lama Muhamad, said voting was a basic right for men and women, but that "this poll does not tell me that the resistance to women's participation has changed."

Al-Jazeera stated that Saudi women resented the way Western media portrayed Arab women as unhappy or oppressed. A female student said: "We are happy. We want to show that image [but] the general image of the Arab woman in the American media is that she is not happy . . . America is trying to force its opinion on us; the change will come from us."

Women in Saudi Arabia are not allowed to drive or travel unless accompanied by a male relative. Human rights advocates say Saudi women are denied equal rights. Some Saudi women resent Western interpretations of their lifestyle.

Racism and the Roma

The right not to experience racism is a fundamental principle of international human rights, but racism continues today in almost every society.

Violent attacks

Since the 1990s the media has reported racist attacks and discrimination against the Roma, particularly in the Czech Republic and Slovakia, formerly Czechoslovakia. The Roma (often incorrectly called gypsies) are the largest ethnic minority in Europe. They live mainly in Central and Eastern Europe.

"Czech Skinheads Escalate Attacks"

In 1998 the *International Herald Tribune* reported that a 26-year-old Roma woman, Helena Bihariova, had been beaten up and thrown unconscious into the Elba River, where she drowned. The newspaper said her "only crime was to be a dark-skinned Czech citizen of Gypsy origin." It said that, according to the human rights group Helsinki Citizens Committee, at least 20 people had been killed in racially motivated attacks in the Czech Republic since 1992. It also said that nearly all of the victims were Romanies. The paper accused "Czech skinheads," describing them as "junior fascists" who regarded Roma as "subhumans."

Much of the world's media, including the BBC, covered the murder. The BBC said Czech politicians reassured "gypsy" leaders that they were trying to take a tougher approach toward racial attacks. Human rights groups said discrimination and racism toward the Roma was widespread. Racism, which views certain ethnic groups as inferior, is one of the most fundamental abuses of human rights.

Improvements?

In 2002 the *Christian Science Monitor* ran the headline: "Czech Roma See Discrimination Beginning to Ebb [lessen]." Its report featured three Romany students who had been accepted into the law faculty of Charles University in Prague, describing their acceptance as "revolutionary." They said: "After centuries of discrimination and isolation, life for the Czech Republic's Romany population appears to be changing for the better." The report also stated: "The extreme nationalistic skinhead movement . . . has been practically driven underground."

The same article said "enormous hurdles" remained. They quoted statistics showing 75 percent of Romany children in special schools for those with learning difficulties and Roma unemployment at 80 percent, as opposed to the national average of 9 percent. They said Romanies were being forced into **ghettos**.

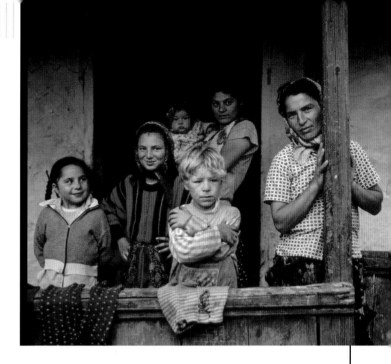

The Roma are spread throughout Central and Eastern Europe. They have been the focus of racist attacks for centuries. Thousands were massacred in the Holocaust during World War II.

In 2005 the French newspaper *Le Monde* reported: "Discrimination of Romanies in the sphere of education and housing is a rule in the Czech Republic . . . racist prejudices are frequent among teachers and even more among local authorities."

What's the truth?

Romano Information, a Czech-based Roma news service, confirms physical attacks have decreased. In 2004 a former Czech skinhead was jailed for 17 years for murdering a Romany man, but reports vary depending on what you read. Human rights observers and Romany websites point to continuing discrimination. Czech government officials say the situation is improving.

WHO'S RIGHT

In July 2004 the Slovak government passed an anti-discrimination law, mainly to safeguard the rights of Slovak Romanies. A few months later, the Slovak Constitutional Court claimed part of the law was unconstitutional because it could be seen as giving preferential treatment to Romanies.

Supporters of the court's decision said: "All Slovak citizens should have the same opportunities and conditions . . . affirmative action or positive discrimination is no better than the negative one." Opponents of the decision called it a "catastrophe," saying, "Everyone who is familiar with the situation of Romanies . . . must know that at least temporary preferential treatment of Romanies is needed."

Expelled from school—for wearing a veil

Many Muslims consider it a duty for women to dress modestly. This is known as *hijab*. It may involve a woman wearing a headscarf known as a *khimar*.

France is a **secular** society, which means that the country does not have an official religion. Church and state are separate, and state schools are free of religion. In 2004 France passed a law banning the wearing of *khimars*, and all other conspicuous religious symbols, in schools. More than 70 female students refused to obey the law and went to school wearing headscarves. A number of them were expelled.

Criticism and defense

The new French law and reactions to it were widely covered by the media. Reports included criticism and support.

Those who criticized the law argued it was a direct attack on France's Muslim population. The BBC reported Muslims saying the law was "a fundamental breach of human rights and intended as a specific attack on their religion." The French Council for the Muslim Religion said: "The spirit and general tone . . . stigmatize [identify in negative terms] one section of the nation, and take no account of the reality of Islam in France."

One of the young women excluded from school commented: "They have just destroyed my life . . . my classmates liked me just the way I was. They didn't ask me to show my hair before electing me class delegate last year."

French President Jacques Chirac defended the law, saying: "The Islamic veil . . . the **kippa** and a cross that is of manifestly excessive dimensions—have no place in the precincts of state schools. State schools will remain secular. For that a law is necessary."

The media network al-Jazeera reported: "Ardent secularists fear the headscarf is an outward sign of a refusal to assimilate fully into French society." A BBC reporter commented that Muslims were **skeptical** about the law's stated aims of keeping schools free of religion. He claimed Muslims saw the law's origins as being "firmly rooted in French fears of an increasingly fundamentalist [strict] form of Islam being practiced by a younger generation of French Muslims."

Whose rights?

Is the law an attack on a person's right to practice his or her religion openly? Or does a secular society have the right to restrict outward expressions of religious faith? Was the law an attack on Muslims? Or were those wearing the veil actively promoting their faith and wishing to remain outside the mainstream? Did expelling schoolgirls who wore the veil deny another human right, the right to an education?

Turkish ban

In 2005 the Turkish government passed a similar law banning the wearing of headscarves in college. They were already banned in schools. The European Court of Human Rights upheld the decision, saying it was justified on the grounds that "there were extremist political movements in Turkey which sought to impose on society as a whole their religious symbols . . . and . . . religious precepts [principles]."

The U.S.-based organization Human Rights Watch attacked the ban and the court's ruling, saying it "clearly infringes the right to religious practice and expression. The European Court has let down thousands of women who will be prevented from studying in Turkey."

In February 2004 the Associated Press reported that thousands of people, many of them women wearing headscarves, marched in protest against the headscarf ban. This woman has added the French word *"fraternité,"* meaning "solidarity," to her headscarf.

Refugee rights: Ship of shame

Refuge and a homeland may seem like fairly basic human rights, but are they? Refugee rights are hotly debated, and media coverage is often distorted or biased.

Seeking asylum

In August 2001 a Norwegian freighter, *MV Tampa*, rescued 438 refugees from an old Indonesian fishing boat stranded off Australia's Christmas Island. Most were from Afghanistan and Iraq. They were seeking asylum in Australia. The Australian government refused the *Tampa* permission to land in Australian waters. After an eight-day "standoff," the refugees were finally taken to a detention center on the island country of Nauru to await a decision on their asylum status.

International interest

The *Tampa* "crisis" provoked interest around the world. The Norwegian government reported the case to the UN, claiming Australia had failed in its responsibilities to asylum seekers and international law. Most Australians supported their government's actions. Australia's prime minister at the time, John Howard, went on to win the general election.

Media coverage

Early media reports stated refugees had threatened to throw their children overboard if they were not granted asylum. A picture was released showing children in the water wearing life jackets. Prime Minister Howard commented: "I certainly don't want people of that type in Australia." The story was later proved false. The so-called evidence was actually a picture taken when the old Indonesian ship was sinking.

Many media reports condemned Australia's actions. The German *Frankfurter Rundschau* described Australia's response as "wrong," "shameful," and "inhuman" and said it marked "a low point in international refugee policy and . . . a breach of the 1951 convention on refugees."

The UK *Independent* said: "Australians should be ashamed . . . the least we can hope of democratically elected political leaders is that they behave with a glimmering of humanity." However, the paper also pointed out: "As many asylum seekers in Britain could testify, Canberra is not alone in making life difficult for those who flee their own country."

The Australian media and government defended the decision. So too did 80 percent of the Australian population. The Australian government claimed they were being "swamped" by refugees and that those on the *Tampa* had been illegally trafficked. The foreign minister launched an attack on "people smugglers . . . gangs who traffick illegally in people," saying Australia wanted to stop "this ugly trade." The prime minister said: "Nobody is lacking in compassion with genuine refugees." He claimed the *Tampa* arrivals were "illegal queue [line] jumpers," trying to avoid the correct procedure for entering Australia.

Unpicking the truth

How can you get to the truth behind the headlines when reports are so contradictory? Is it possible to decide whose rights are being defended? There are at least 14 million refugees in the world today needing asylum, and there is international and media pressure on many governments to do something about it. Applying the pressure may distort the truth.

Under an Australian migration policy nicknamed "the Pacific Solution," asylum seekers are held in detention centers on Pacific Islands until their cases have been heard. This young Iraqi boy and his father are survivors of a ship wrecked while sailing from Indonesia to Australia. Over 350 other asylum seekers lost their lives when it sank.

Israeli forces have raided and destroyed thousands of Palestinian homes. They claim they are hunting out militants, who are a threat to Israel's security. Palestinians claim that the Israeli raids are deliberate aggression and violate their fundamental human right to live and have shelter.

Conflict in Palestine

The Palestinian conflict is a long-running dispute between Israel and the Palestinians. Many Palestinians were displaced from their homes when the state of Israel was created in 1948. Both sides claim that Palestine is their homeland, and over the years there has been a great deal of violence between the two sides.

Security fence or apartheid wall?

In 2002 the Israeli government began building a wall on the West Bank to divide Israel from Palestinian occupied territory. Their stated aim was to physically separate the West Bank from Israel and so prevent suicide bombing attacks on Israel. The first stage was completed in July 2003. It stretched for 90 miles (145 kilometers) and consisted of walls, electrified fences, trenches, and watchtowers. In some places, the wall extends 4 miles (6.4 kilometers) into Palestinian territory, thereby preventing Palestinians from accessing farming land, schools, and water supplies.

The Israeli government says the wall is a "security fence" and necessary to stop Palestinian suicide bombers. It says the wall is temporary and follows the "green line"—an **armistice** line between Israel and Palestine established in 1949.

Palestinians call it an "apartheid" wall. They argue that it does not follow the green line and engulfs Palestinian towns and villages. They say Israel is annexing (taking over) Palestinian territory.

In July 2004 the UN's high court, the International Court of Justice (ICJ), ruled that Israel's fence violated international law and should be dismantled. The UN General Assembly adopted a resolution demanding that Israel comply with the decision.

Media coverage

The Israeli wall attracted worldwide media attention. Al-Jazeera and other Arab media demanded an end to the building of the wall. Former Palestinian leader Yasser Arafat said: "Right now the Israelis do whatever they want . . . their sole aim is to destroy us." *Islam Online* quoted from a report presented to the UN by John Dugard, an expert on human rights in the occupied territories. He said: "The time has come to condemn the wall as an unlawful act of annexation."

The Israeli press criticized the UN expert's report, saying it was "one-sided, highly politicized, and biased" and "totally disregarded the deaths of 900 Israelis in attacks since September 2000."

The Arab media and the European press welcomed the World Court ruling. President Bush was reported as saying: "I think the wall is a problem. It is very difficult to develop confidence between the Palestinians and Israelis with a wall snaking through the West Bank." However, the Bush administration expressed disappointment with the World Court ruling and challenged its authority. A spokesman for the White House stated: "We do not believe that it is the appropriate forum to resolve what is a political issue."

Amnesty International recognized "Israel's legitimate need to prevent access to people who might constitute a threat to its security." However, it said it would have "severe negative consequences" for Palestinian human rights, such as the right to food, medical care, and an adequate standard of living.

Who decides?

You will find numerous websites on the Arab-Israeli conflict and its human rights issues. Discovering the truth behind news coverage and deciding whose rights should be upheld— and how—is perhaps more difficult on this issue than many others. Some people have said it is almost impossible for the media to present an **objective** report. Both sides have such deeply held feelings, they will either see media reports as biased or use the media to put their side across.

In 2005 the then-Israeli Prime Minister Ariel Sharon announced Israeli settlers on the Gaza Strip were to be evacuated. Many settlers resisted, claiming they had been "betrayed" and had a fundamental right to live there.

Children are unbeatable

Children have rights separate from adults. This is a fairly new idea. The Convention on the Rights of the Child was issued in 1990. Since then every country has ratified it, except the United States and Somalia.

Children's rights are based on the principle that "in all actions concerning children . . . the best interests of the child shall be a primary consideration." Who, though, decides what is in the "best interests" of a child?

Many adults think they should have the right to hit their children, and that it is not a matter for national or international laws. What do you think?

No ban on hitting

In 2004 the UK House of Commons rejected a complete ban on parents being allowed to hit their children. Most MPs (members of parliament, the main legislative body in the UK) supported the view that parents had the right to discipline their children using "moderate" hitting. The general view was that punishment would not be "reasonable" if it left a mark on a child's body.

The arguments

Anti-hitting campaigners claimed that according to their figures, 71 percent of the British public supported an outright ban. In contrast, figures produced by the British government's Office of National Statistics found that 88 percent of people thought it is sometimes necessary to hit a child.

The media covered the debate in the House of Commons and reported differing opinions. Theresa May, a Conservative Party MP, rejected the total ban. She said ministers should avoid "trying to tell people how to run their lives. We all know there is a limit beyond which parents should not go and at the point where what is reasonable control actually becomes abuse. That obviously is wrong and government and society has a right to step in at that point."

A spokesperson for British Prime Minister Tony Blair said he did "not believe there should be a law banning parents from [hitting] their children." Iain Bainbridge, a Christian Institute development officer, said: "It's wrong to criminalize parents for using moderate physical punishment."

Lucy Thorpe, policy adviser for the NSPCC (the National Society for the Prevention of Cruelty to Children), argued for a complete ban. She said: "What we are talking about here is children having the same protection as adults under the law on assault . . . the discussion is often based on 'what harm does a light [hit] do?' It may do no physical harm, but there are several things attached . . . it sends a clear message to children that might is right . . .we would not accept for a wife or husband to give their partner a [hit] and it should be the same for children."

The Liberal Democrat Party's spokesperson, Annette Brooke, also supported a ban. She said that other European countries had introduced a ban and "evidence . . . shows that such a rule not only protects children but has also brought about a change in culture towards children."

Who decides?
Adults made this decision, and usually make all decisions. The media did not report children's views. Do you think children and young people should be contributing to the debate on this children's rights issue?

ILLEGAL

By December 2005 the following countries or territories had banned physical punishment in the home: Austria, Bulgaria, Croatia, Cyprus, Denmark, Finland, Germany, Hungary, Iceland, Israel, Italy, Latvia, Portugal, Romania, Sweden, Ukraine, Norway (including Spitzbergen), Pitcairn Islands (a UK dependency).

The NSPCC is the UK's leading charity specializing in the prevention of cruelty to children. This image comes from a campaign encouraging people to speak openly when they know child abuse is taking place.

Street children: Who's responsible?
Murder in Honduras
In 2001 a UN human rights investigator called on the Honduran government to prevent the "extrajudicial [illegal] killing of hundreds of children and teenagers." According to reports by Casa Alianza, a non-governmental organization (NGO), more than 800 young people had been murdered since 1998 in what they described as a policy of "social cleansing." They claimed the killings were part of a deliberate social policy known as *"mano duro"* (strong hand). This aimed to clear the streets of groups—particularly street gangs and street children—that the government and police consider to be "social vermin" and "criminals."

The Honduran press, some international press, and human rights groups covered the UN visit, but there was little coverage overall.

Denied human rights
An estimated 20,000 children and young people live on the streets of Honduras, and every year hundreds die. They leave their families for many reasons, such as poverty, abuse, or family break-up. Sometimes war or natural disasters mean parents can no longer support their children. Street children make a small living on the streets, but are constantly at risk because they are deprived of basic human rights such as shelter, security, and protection from violence. Many of these young people are physically abused or murdered, and their situation is often unreported.

One young Honduran girl told human rights workers that "if you turn up dead someday, no one is going to wonder how you died."

Is the state involved?
In 2001 Andres Pavon of the Committee for the Defense of Human Rights in Honduras said: "There have been many killings . . . those responsible are gang members . . . a percentage of them have been state agents."

Casa Alianza said police were murdering street children. The police denied responsibility. They blamed gang rivalries. The Honduran government admitted police may have been responsible, but insisted they were isolated cases that would be punished.

A year later little had happened. Casa Alianza accused the Honduran government of showing no interest in solving the murders. A UN official asked: "How is it possible that in this country every day armed people kill children and young people and the security forces don't capture anyone and don't know who are the executioners?"

The Honduran president at the time, Ricardo Maduro, promised a policy of "zero-tolerance" and sent more than 8,000 soldiers and police into the city. The security minister said: "We are going to clear up once and for all who is carrying out these killings of children and young people." The killings continued, however, and 64 children were killed in December 2002 alone.

Urgent appeals

In 2003 and 2004 Amnesty International launched worldwide appeals calling on the Honduran government to investigate and bring the killers of children to justice. Around 2,300 children had been murdered. The Honduran government had set up a special unit, but despite promises, only 400 cases had been investigated, and only three had resulted in a conviction.

News coverage

Interestingly, there has been little media reporting on the murder of Honduran street children. Their lifestyle is often highlighted. Street children are forced to turn to crime, drugs, and prostitution in order to survive on the streets. However, their murders are not headline news. Does their lifestyle mean they have no human rights?

There are thousands of children like these living on the streets in Honduras. They pick up casual work or survive through crime and prostitution. Hundreds have been raped, tortured, and murdered by police and security forces.

Sold into slavery

The slave trade was banned a long time ago. You may think it is over—but is it?

A mysterious ship

In 2001 a story appeared in the media that grabbed world headlines. A Nigerian registered ship, the *MV Etireno*, was refused permission to dock in Gabon, on the west coast of Africa. Reports claimed there were 250 children on board who had been sold into slavery. For a while the ship disappeared. Dramatic claims appeared in the press, including a suggestion that the ship's captain might throw children overboard to avoid detection. **UNICEF** and non-governmental organizations (NGOs) were increasingly concerned for the children's safety. Finally, the ship docked in Benin, in western Africa, where police, welfare agencies, and UN representatives were waiting. Initial reports were confusing, but it was confirmed that among the various passengers were 43 children and young people.

Was it a slave ship?

International news reports carried contradictory claims . . .

The Namibian claimed: "Far from being children facing a life of slavery, most passengers aboard the ship . . . were desperately trying to find work in oil-rich Gabon." They quoted one young man who said, "I was looking for work," and said the ship was turned back from Gabon "because . . . it was carrying would-be illegal immigrants."

CNN covered the events extensively. The ship's captain said, "I have not committed any offense. I am not into child slavery, they cannot prove it." The ship's owner, a Nigerian soccer star, also denied involvement, saying, "I bought [the ship] to help create jobs for the unemployed youths in Nigeria . . . I'm not into any dubious [questionable] dealings."

Millions of children and young people worldwide are forced to work in slave-like conditions. Some work in sweatshops, producing consumer goods for Western countries. Many girls and young women are trafficked across borders and forced into prostitution or pornography.

UNICEF, anti-slavery NGOs, and aid agency *Terre des Hommes* disagreed. They claimed that the children had been sold into slavery. They reported: "Five of the 43 children and youths . . . said their families were each paid 10,000 CFA [a local currency] before their departure. Eight other children confirmed having traveled with unknown intermediaries on board ship."

Exposing slavery
Although reports were confusing, some important facts emerged. The high-profile coverage of the *Etireno* helped to highlight a slave trade that UNICEF and others had known about for some time.

UNICEF says at least 200,000 children are traded into slavery every year in west and central Africa. Poverty is the cause. Desperately poor families sell their children for between $1.50 and $14 each. Traffickers then sell them for a profit. Children end up on coffee, cocoa, and cotton plantations. Many end up as domestic workers or prostitutes, sometimes in Europe.

What comes first?
Countries around the world have agreed to protect children's rights. Slavery is illegal. Can children's rights to security and freedom from abuse be protected or enforced where extreme poverty exists?

Privacy vs. safety

Laws in many countries safeguard some important rights, including our rights to privacy, to protest, and to voice our opinions. Yet these rights are routinely abused in countries with highly oppressive regimes. Democracies pride themselves on safeguarding these basic human rights, but are there times when national security comes before individual privacy?

New laws

Since the terrorist attacks of September 11, 2001, many countries have passed anti-terrorist laws. These laws enable authorities to gather and retain electronic data in order to prevent, investigate, or detect serious criminal acts, including terrorism. For example, in 2001 the U.S. government passed the Patriot Act, which gave sweeping powers to the intelligence services. Spain, Belgium, Australia, and other countries have passed similar anti-terrorist legislation that enables the retention of electronic data.

Privacy is hard to maintain in an electronic age. Governments, police, and commercial companies hold considerable amounts of data about most people. The question is whether governments should be able to access personal correspondence as a safeguard against possible terrorist threats.

In December 2005 the *New York Times* published a report providing evidence that the U.S. National Security Agency (NSA) had been wiretapping phone calls and emails from within the United States without obtaining a court-approved warrant. Sometime after September 11, 2001, President Bush had told the NSA it did not need to obtain warrants for these searches.

Important tool or snoop laws?

This wiretapping became controversial. Many legal scholars argued that U.S. law requires that the government obtain a court-approved warrant before beginning any wiretapping. Civil liberties groups such as the American Civil Liberties Union (ACLU) quickly demanded an explanation. The Bush administration argued, however, that the right to secretly wiretap fell within the president's "inherent powers," especially in light of the war on terror after September 11, 2001. In June 2006 the *New York Times* issued another report, this time revealing that the Treasury Department had been secretly monitoring bank records of suspected terrorists. This, too, quickly ignited controversy.

As with the previous report in 2005, the Bush administration stated that it was wrong of the *New York Times* to publish such information, claiming it hurt its efforts to stop terrorism. Others argued that such reports fell within the freedom of the press, and that Americans had a right to know when their civil liberties were being violated. These and similar measures enacted by the U.S. government have aroused strong feelings, which have been voiced through the media and elsewhere.

Infringement or necessary safeguard?

People in a democracy expect their privacy to be protected. Can special circumstances—such as the threat of terrorist attacks—override civil liberties and human rights? Spanish and UK authorities claim data collection helped the police after the Madrid and London bombings. U.S. and Spanish authorities say data collection has helped prevent other attacks.

Human rights advocates argue the new laws are an infringement of human rights and open to abuse. They say a democracy must safeguard hard-won civil liberties. Who is right and who decides?

Standing up for democracy

Some human rights events are so dramatic that they are overwhelming. Getting to the truth can be challenging.

For seven weeks from April until June 1989, thousands and perhaps millions of Chinese students and workers demonstrated in and around Beijing, China. The reasons for the protest varied, but included a demand for freedom of the press and an end to government corruption. The demonstrators occupied Tiananmen Square, and hundreds went on hunger strike. As protests and demonstrations grew, the Chinese government declared **martial law**. The Chinese government sent troops and tanks to clear the square and crush the protest. Violence broke out, leading to civilian and army deaths.

Media coverage

The world's press was already in China to cover a visit by former Soviet leader Mikhail Gorbachev. Coverage of Tiananmen Square and its suppression dominated the news as CNN and others relayed events as they occurred.

Differing views

A declassified U.S. State Department document dated June 1989 said: "How the government of [the People's Republic of China] . . . decides to deal with those of its citizens involved in recent events is . . . an internal affair. How [the U.S. and] . . .the American people view that activity is . . . an internal affair. Both will be governed by the traditions, culture and values peculiar to each." Is that how everyone sees the issues?

Reports in the Western media were very sympathetic to the demonstrators, describing their protest as a "pro-democracy" movement. The United States and other Western governments condemned the way the protest was suppressed. Media reports described it as a "massacre" or "bloody" military operation. There were graphic accounts of brutality and descriptions of injured students in the hospital. The U.S. president at the time, George H. W. Bush, said he deeply condemned the use of force.

The Chinese press—the *People's Daily*—accused the students and protestors of plotting to cause turmoil. They were presented as "troublemakers" out to "disrupt the social order." Meanwhile, Chinese government officials censored and controlled the media coverage of events so that many rural Chinese did not know what was happening. Chinese officials also limited access for foreign media. They denied reports of a massacre.

Whose truth?

There are many articles, books, and websites on the Tiananmen Square protest. Some have criticized the international press for being too emotional and not objective. Yet for many people in Western democracies, Tiananmen Square was seen as an abuse of a basic human right—the right to protest and express an opinion.

China is a communist country, not a democracy. The Chinese government viewed the protest differently from people in the West. It saw the protest as a threat to the existing social order and argued that the protesters were troublemakers. The Chinese government was surprised by Western reactions. During the "Cultural Revolution" in the 1960s, thousands of Chinese were killed, imprisoned, or humiliated, but there had been little Western criticism.

HOW MANY DEAD?

Western media reported that 2,600 to 3,000 were killed in the Tiananmen Square protest. The Chinese government said 300. Exact figures have never been released.

This lone Chinese protester briefly halted the advancing tanks. The image flashed around the world. Western media do not know his name or what happened to him. Some claim he was executed; others say he is in hiding.

YOU NEED TO DECIDE

Human rights issues are complicated. Media reports on human rights can be difficult to unravel. Governments, states, and individuals often have very different opinions.

THINK ABOUT THESE QUESTIONS

- Do you agree that we should all have basic human rights?
- How far have human rights progressed since 1948?
- Are some groups of people denied rights?
- Do different countries recognize the same rights?
- Are some rights more important than others?
- How can human rights be enforced?
- Who decides whether a right should be enforced or not?
- Is the UN the best way forward for human rights?
- Can one country impose rights on another?
- Can human rights be changed depending on circumstances?
- Can different cultures and societies ever reach agreement on human rights?
- Which are more important—economic or political human rights?
- Can the media be trusted to present an accurate view?
- Is democracy the first step toward achieving human rights?

How would you answer these questions? Can you find out more in other books and magazines, through the media, or on the Internet to back up your views?

The day the United Nations Universal Declaration of Human Rights was issued— December 10—is Human Rights Day. In 1998, on the 50th anniversary of the Declaration, millions of people worldwide signed a petition in support of universal human rights.

Human rights are a hotly debated major political issue. They are also a rallying point for people who are oppressed or discriminated against.

You need to know what your rights are and you need to respect other people's rights. One day you may have to vote on a new law or make other important decisions that affect not only your rights, but also the rights of someone else. Where can you find information to help you make that decision? If you use the media, how will you decide what the truth is? Can you separate out fact from opinion?

Human rights are not selfish. They are about taking responsibility for ourselves and for each other. They are values and principles that can help to decide how we live our lives. They need to be protected and promoted. In today's world, respect for human rights may be the only way to resolve conflict, poverty, and oppression.

Human rights are now taught in many schools. Students are encouraged to learn about rights and how they can be applied not only to individuals, but also collectively.

TIMELINE

1215
Magna Carta, England: Barons and nobles begin to define their rights and limit the powers of the king.

1775–1783
American Revolution leads to independence from Britain and establishment of the United States of America.

1787
U.S. Constitution is written. The Bill of Rights, added in 1791, guaranteed Americans' basic rights, such as freedom of speech and religion.

1789
French Revolution breaks out, leading to the overthrow of the monarchy. A National Assembly issues a Declaration of the Rights of Man, which lays out democratic principles and states that all "men" have equal rights.

1792
British feminist Mary Wollstonecraft publishes *Vindication of the Rights of Woman*, in which she argues for equal rights for women.

1848
First women's rights convention in Seneca Falls, New York.

1893
Women in New Zealand are the first in the world to gain equal voting rights with men. In the U.S., not until 1920 does the passage of the 19th amendment give women the right to vote.

1914–1918
World War I.

1919
League of Nations founded, the forerunner of the United Nations.

1939–1945
World War II. The liberation of concentration camps at the end of the war reveals the atrocities of the Holocaust.

1945
United Nations (UN) comes into existence.

1945–1946
Nazi leaders are tried at Nuremberg, Germany, for "crimes against humanity."

1948
UN issues Universal Declaration of Human Rights. Forty-eight member states are signatories. Convention on the Prevention and Punishment of Genocide adopted (in force 1951).

1951
Convention Relating to the Status of Refugees.

1961
Amnesty International founded to focus attention on "political prisoners" worldwide.

1966
International Covenant on Civil and Political Rights and International Covenant on Economic, Social, and Cultural rights (in force 1976).

1967
UN introduces first sanctions against South Africa's apartheid regime. Israel occupies the Gaza Strip during the Six Day War; many more Palestinians become refugees.

1969
Convention on the Elimination of All Forms of Racial Discrimination.

1973
Augusto Pinochet seizes power in Chile, leading to death squads and "disappearances" (murders) of political opponents.

1976
Amnesty International awarded Nobel Peace Prize. UN Human Rights Committee set up.

1978
U.S.-based human rights organization, Human Rights Watch, founded to highlight human rights abuses worldwide.

1979
Convention on the Elimination of All Forms of Discrimination against Women adopted (in force 1981).

1980s
Human rights activists worldwide boycott South African goods in a campaign against apartheid.

1987
Convention Against Torture.

1989
Convention on the Rights of the Child adopted (in force 1990). The fall of Berlin Wall ends communism in Eastern Europe.

c. 1991
Apartheid ends in South Africa.

1994
Genocide in Rwanda.

1995
Serbian army massacres Bosnians in Srebrenica.

1998
Pinochet, former president of Chile, charged with allegations of systematic torture of Chilean citizens.

1998
102 nations agree a statute to establish an International Criminal Court (ICC). Seven nations oppose it, including the United States, China, Libya, Iran, and Saudi Arabia.

2001
Terrorist attacks on New York and the Pentagon. U.S. forces invade Afghanistan.

2002
International Criminal Court (ICC) established.

2003
U.S.-led forces invade Iraq.

2005
Former Iraqi leader Saddam Hussein brought to trial.

GLOSSARY

administration government, but particularly the executives who carry out the work of government

allege to accuse someone of wrongdoing without having yet proved it

al-Qaeda (also al-Qaida) Islamic fundamentalist group or network seeking to end Western influence on Islamic affairs

Amnesty International largest human rights group in the world

apartheid political system in South Africa that existed from 1948 to c. 1991. It separated black people from white people and gave privileges to white people. The word "apartheid" comes from the Afrikaans word meaning "separation."

armistice truce in war

asylum safe place where people can go

atrocity shocking, cruel act

bias showing a strong dislike of or preference for something

censor to take something out of a publication, such as a newspaper, to prevent it from being known

civil liberties basic personal rights of an individual, guaranteed by law, such as freedom of speech

civil rights rights of citizens to freedom and equality

Cold War name given to the period 1948–1991, a time of political tension between the former Soviet Union and other communist states and the United States and its capitalist allies. The two superpowers did not fight each other directly, but backed opposing sides in various conflicts.

collude plan or work together

constitution written statement or document setting out the fundamental laws or principles of a country or organization

constitutional according to a country's constitution

contravene to break a law or rule

customary international law law that becomes binding because it is followed according to custom. It is not written, but becomes "law by use."

democracy country governed by representatives who have been voted into power by the people of that country

deterrent something that stops (deters) something from happening

discrimination unfair treatment of a person or group of people

due process right of a citizen to proper legal procedures

economic sanction when a country uses economic means to force change in another country, such as not buying goods from that country

extraordinary rendition process by which terrorist suspects can be taken and rendered (transferred) to other countries for questioning. This process operates outside legal or court procedure.

Geneva Convention international agreement, adopted in 1949, that lays down rules about how prisoners of war should be treated

genocide systematic killing of all the people in a national, ethnic, or religious group, or an attempt to do this

ghetto separate area within a town or city where people of a particular ethnic group may gather and live together, or be forced to

interrogate to question someone thoroughly, and often aggressively, perhaps in a jail or courtroom

kippa head covering worn by Jews

legislation law or laws

martial law military control and policing

media television, newspapers, radio, magazines—all the various forms of mass communication

objective free of bias or prejudice

persistent vegetative state (PVS) medical condition in which someone's brain is so badly damaged that he or she cannot stay alive without a life-support system

preamble section at the beginning of a speech or document

propaganda information put out by a government or organization to promote or encourage a particular idea or viewpoint

racism prejudice against people who belong to a particular race, based on a belief that one race is superior to another

ratify accept. If a state ratifies a human rights treaty, it is bound by the treaty.

refugee person who has been forced to flee his or her country because of war or persecution

Roma ethnic group that lives throughout Central and Eastern Europe. Sometimes incorrectly called gypsies.

secular not religious. A secular society does not follow any particular religious rules.

Sharia Muslim code of religious law

skeptical doubting ideas, beliefs, or information

slant to present something, such as a news item, in a biased or prejudiced way

Taliban political and military force that ruled Afghanistan from 1996 to 2001. Includes mujahedin (holy warriors).

trafficking illegal trade—for example, of drugs or people

UNICEF (sometimes Unicef) United Nations Children's Fund

unlawful combatant someone who is not given the legal rights that a soldier should have during war

violate to deny someone's legal rights, or to act contrary to a law

FIND OUT MORE

Books

Brownlie, Ali. *Exploring Tough Issues: Why Do People Abuse Human Rights?* Chicago: Raintree, 2005.

Kramer, Ann. *Mandela: The Rebel Who Led His Nation to Freedom.* Washington, D.C.: National Geographic, 2005.

Ross, Stewart. *Witness to History: The Arab-Israeli Conflict.* Chicago: Heinemann Library, 2004.

Ross, Stewart. *World Watch: United Nations.* Chicago: Raintree, 2004.

Smith, Dan. *The Penguin State of the World Atlas.* New York: Penguin, 2003.

Stand Up for Your Rights. Chicago: World Book, 1998.
A book about human rights—written, illustrated, and edited by young people of the world.

Useful websites

There are lots of websites on the Internet dealing with human rights. You can use a search engine to look up whichever topic interests you.

Some websites that might be useful include:

The United Nations
http://www.un.org/
UN Universal Declaration of Human Rights
http://www.un.org/Overview/rights.html
Human rights overview
http://www.hrweb.org/legal/undocs.html
Convention on the Rights of the Child
http://www.unhchr.ch/html/menu3/b/k2crc.htm
Amnesty International
http://www.amnesty.org/
Human Rights Watch
http://www.hrw.org/
Death penalty: Facts and figures
http://web.amnesty.org/pages/deathpenalty-facts-eng
Q & A about the death penalty
http://www.amnestyusa.org/abolish/dp_qa.html
Death penalty in the United States
http://www.deathpenaltyinfo.org/

Torture: Summary of international laws prohibiting torture
http://www.hrw.org/english/docs/2004/05/24/usint8614.htm

Equality Now: Campaigning group for the rights of women
http://www.equalitynow.org/english/
Minority rights
http://www.minorityrights.org/
The state of the world's children: UNICEF advance report 2006
http://www.unicef.org/sowc06/intro.html

Activities

Here are some ideas for finding out more about human rights.

- Take a look at the clothes you're wearing—your jeans, sneakers, or sweatshirt. Where were they made? Who made them, and what were the workers paid? What were their working conditions like? Do you think their rights were being met?

- Do you know what your rights are? Find out what rights you have in your country. How are they guaranteed? What can you do in your country if your rights are abused? Decide how well you think human rights are protected or promoted in your country.

- Make a list of what you think are the most important human rights. Put them in order. How do they compare with the UN Universal Declaration of Human Rights? Can you think of human rights that ought to be added? For instance, what about freedom from pollution?

- Talk about human rights. There may be issues that you've read about in this book or you've seen in the media. Talk about them with your friends. Look at both sides of the question. Perhaps organize a class debate at school.

- Get involved. There are many ways to get involved in human rights campaigns. Decide which particular issue interests you most, or which you think is most important. Look it up on the Internet. Find out if there's an NGO campaigning on that issue and what they need you to do. You might write letters, draw up a petition, or set up an exhibition.

- Find out more. Human rights activists have risked their lives and safety to campaign for human rights. They have been censored, imprisoned, and even killed. Find out who they are. You could start by looking up the following:

    Mordecai Vanunu, in prison for revealing Israeli nuclear secrets.

    Ken Saro-Wiwa, executed in Nigeria for rights campaigns.

    Aung San Suu Kyi, Burmese fighter for democracy.

    Rigoberto Menchú, Guatemalan campaigner for the rights of indigenous (native) peoples.

INDEX